Foreword

The essay contained in this volume discusses some principles applicable to research management. The author, who is head of the Research Unit, places them in the context of the consideration of the objectives of criminological research and how both can be related to the needs of government.

OLIVER SIMPSON
Chief Scientist

March 1981

Contents

Managing Criminological Research

Introduction

In discussing the hero of Turgenev's novel *Fathers and Sons*, Sir Isaiah Berlin[1] remarks that "Bazarov's faith rested on the claim that the dissection of frogs was more important than poetry because it led to the truth, whereas the poetry of Pushkin did not". In a later work the same author, in discussing the liberal position between extreme right and extreme left, takes up the theme again. "In a sense, the Bazarovs have won. The victorious advance of quantitative methods, belief in the organisation of life by technological management, reliance on nothing but calculation of utilitarian consequences in evaluating policies that affect vast numbers of human beings, this is Bazarov, not the Kirsanovs".

This essay is concerned with two aspects of that theme. First, a commentary on 'technological management' as applied to the problem of crime; and second, some consideration of how that management might operate.

To an extent, the elaboration of these aspects skirts ground that has been covered in two previous contributions to this series. An earlier report[2] argued that, since crime is a relative concept, the process of formulating a research programme intended to influence policy must be flexible. Faced with the reality of crime, social scientists, administrators and practitioners needed to agree on common objectives. The study emphasised the place of research in the assessment of resources allocated to the criminal justice system, and which within limits are controlled by government.

A subsequent report[3] returned to the subject of the relationship of research to policy. It did not attempt to enquire in any detail into how change came about in criminal policy, or the exact part played by criminological or penological research. The purpose was rather to expose some of the considerations which affect this process. It was argued that, if policy were to be influenced, conceptual ideas about crime must "harmonise with or, at best avoid conflict with, other conceptions of crime" which are derived from sources other than research. Only if the results of research were presented to the policy maker in a form that could be related to practical solutions at a reasonable cost, carried out within a reasonable time span, would they be likely to affect policy. The history of the formulation of criminal policy showed that some issues, being fundamental to a democratic society, would always feature in that formulation. Other problems, too, tended to be perennial so that current policy

1

concerns were not necessarily peculiar to this decade; what had changed was not their essence but the emphasis and focus given them. However, the study also recognised that, in addition to conventional categories of crime, technological development had fostered a new category involving both the public and private domain which was likely to pose problems for crime control and crime reduction. If research were to maintain its close ties with criminal policy, it was incumbent on social scientists to keep this wider context in prospect: a task potentially more rewarding in its evaluation of wider policy options than merely the day-to-day monitoring of the criminal justice system.

For the purpose of this essay, the arena selected for the exploration of technological management is again criminological research and its bearing on criminal and penal policy. But the notion of such management implied in the opening paragraph is applicable to other social sciences and their relevance to social policy, and the argument that follows is presented in the belief that it may be of interest to those active in other fields of human endeavour, which are also the concern of government.

Crime as a problem to be solved
Many people, perhaps most people, perceive crime as a phenomenon that, given the resources and the will, could be eradicated. Although there may be extenuating circumstances in which some people commit some crimes, crime is often (in some societies, generally) equated with sin. Whether or not there is absolute justification, in the logical sense, for taking this view, there are historical reasons for this outlook — which is intrinsic to the Judaeo-Christian tradition. Crime is also seen as a disease which, if the cause and hence the cure could be found, is capable of elimination. While this stance from the moral point of view is difficult to assail, it is not so defensible in scientific terms. The medical analogy of crime as equivalent to disease is misleading. The evidence suggests that both the concept and the measurable incidence of crime has varied historically and varies geographically. Contemporary estimates of its extent fluctuate according to political and cultural patterns, and even within modern times in some countries its prevalence has ebbed and flowed.

The Victorians, in fact, came very near to solving the problem of crime as conceived in the terms of that age. The high water mark of this achievement was reached towards the end of the nineteenth century in England and its effects seem to have been perpetuated to about the middle of the present century. How this came about is a matter of historical assessment.[4] The combination of increased efficiency on the part of the police, the courts and the penal system, and increased co-operation by the public with the law and those who enforced it, seemingly produced a real reduction in the crime rate. No doubt other factors were involved, notably the operation of the Poor Law, the spread of elementary education and perhaps the provision of institutions of one sort or another for the mentally defective. And unlike the United

States of America, at least, material progress[5] did not go hand in hand with an increasing crime rate. Fascinating as further speculation along this path may be, it is not the purpose of this essay to pursue it.[6] The focus of the inquiry is narrower — it is not so much the solution of the problem of crime as the conceptual approach to that task, and what assistance — in the present day — is provided by the social scientist to the policy maker. At the beginning of the century, criminology was hardly a recognised subject of academic study in this country, and it was not until the early nineteen thirties that much progress was made in this regard. With the apparent increase in crime which has characterised the last thirty years, the aid of criminology has been invoked by policy makers on an increasing scale. Criminological research, however, has not solved the problem of crime and, in so far as this research is an element of technological management. such management in the sense that Turgenev's hero conceived it — has been a failure. This prompts several questions: can research solve problems? Is crime, indeed, a soluble problem? Whether it is, or not, are the right issues being tackled by research in the best way?

It is doubtful whether criminological research can solve problems. The order of problems, and the means to tackle it, are quite different from questions such as how a man could land on the moon or diphtheria be eradicated. The positivist approach which informed much criminological research in the middle of this century was not of itself wrong, in the sense of being unscientific. Expectations were too high and the available techniques and skills were often applied to unsuitable issues. There was a mismatch between the expectations of those who commissioned research, the objectives of the investigations themselves and the available technology. In these circumstances, it has been difficult to maintain the credibility of criminological research — at least, as an aid to policy formation — through almost three decades. Crime, like many other aspects of human behaviour, is a complex phenomenon. The term, as a collective noun, is itself misleading because the subject is much better approached as a discrete series of events: not crime, but crimes. While there is some certain knowledge, there is a great deal that remains to be learned about the phenomenon; furthermore the phenomenon, or for preference the phenomena, are not constants. The extent of intellectual investment in the discipline is considerably less than in some other social sciences, and certainly in the natural sciences. With limited means, and a certain insufficiency of basic descriptive data upon which to draw, it is unlikely that particular pieces of research can solve particular problems and, with confidence, be applied to the development of a particular policy. The aims must of necessity be more modest and, if criminological research has achieved anything in recent years, it has helped to destroy popular myths about the causes and consequences of crimes, to expose the complexity of the problems facing those whose concern is the enforcement of the law, and to suggest options less for the positive commitment of resources than for the avoidance of the dissipation of such resources.

3

In the formulation of aims for research lies a difficulty central to the subject and which was not sufficiently recognised[8] when, in the sixth decade of this century, criminological research was first invoked in any systematic way as an aid to policy formation. This concerns the ideological context in which research is conducted. The issue of power in the control of crime, who uses it and how; and its effects on those it attempts to constrain, cannot be ignored. It is not easy to disassociate independent scientific inquiry from ideology. For example, if there is any truth in the proposition that crime is the price of freedom, then some investigation is required of those parts of the world where freedom obtains without the adjunct of crime; and furthermore, whereas in most industrialised societies of the West crime is prevalent, a closer look at the exact relationship between economic and industrial development and criminal activity is warranted. Socialist countries claim that not only are their societies relatively crime free but the correlation between any increase in crime and an increase in industrial output is not necessarily positive. Unfortunately, because the measures used to relate crime and other indicators of social and economic function are not as accurate as they at first appear, and the whole subject is beset with problems of determining causal relationships, more investigation seems to be required before one can venture on the beckoning but fairly uncharted seas of cross-national and cultural comparative research. It may turn out, of course, that political and social structures[9] do hold a key to the control of crime — but this in turn raises even wider questions about the relationship of criminal to social policy; at this stage such speculation without firmer evidence is idle.

It is not only in the consideration of liberty, which is the point made by Sir Isaiah Berlin in the passage quoted in the introduction to this essay, but in addressing the characteristics of social justice or the relation of criminal to social policy that one immediately comes up against the problem of what the proper objective of research ought to be. It is something of a dilemma and danger for criminology because, if the Bazarovs of this world were going to have a field day in any subject, surely this offers one of the more inviting prospects.[10] Within the traditions of scientific method as practised in the Western world, however, they have not yet succeeded. Because of this failure, perhaps, criminology remains an humane science.

Consensus about the definition of legitimate areas of inquiry, the aims of research and the limitations of what research can achieve is desirable if those who commission it are not going to be disappointed with or disillusioned by the result. As an instrument of the technological management of crime — and this is not its exclusive function — research has a role to play but one that is dependent on the capability of the actors, the technical resources of the management, the capacity of the theatre and the appreciation of the audience. If this conclusion is seen as pessimistic, it is only intended as an antidote to optimistic claims that have been made. There is scope enough for research if the constraints are understood.

4

The application of technological management

The incorporation of research in policy making, and the manner of achieving it — the amount of investment, the remit and status of the organisation which is charged with carrying out the work, and its place in the institutions of government — reflect the value put on the exercise. Although there are differences, which are a function of governmental structures and attitudes, in the organisation of criminological research in different countries, there appear to be some common features — whether the location is London, Paris or the Hague; Canberra or Ottawa; Washington or indeed Moscow, to mention some of the principal capitals where sizeable official capabilities of one sort or another exist for the furtherance of research in criminal justice. This is a subject which, although there is a paucity of relevant published material,[11] tends to receive increasing attention at conferences and in journals devoted to the analysis of policy.

Ideal conditions for research are rarely realised. The nature of the activity is such that originality and inventiveness flourish better without distraction, and sufficient leisure is desirable to pursue lines of thought and inquiry that may be far removed from first intention. If it contains an element of serendipity, routine and indeed drudgery also feature largely. The social scientist's equivalent of the natural scientist's laboratory experiment is field work, and can be equally diverting. It is often necessary for the research worker to set himself, or to be set by his supervisor, limited objectives if he is not to be overwhelmed by more information than can be satisfactorily analysed. The research worker, furthermore, is subject to various distractions, or alternative commitments, that cannot be ignored: in universities, teaching; in govern-ment, demands for advice and subservience to bureaucratic procedures that characterise large organisations; and in research institutes, the pressure to attract the next contract while completing the last one.

The career of the research worker, too, is not one that is recognised by particular security of tenure or, to an extent, by progressive remuneration. Often he may reach more or less his maximum level of income within the space of a few years to find that, unless he seeks opportunities in research management, teaching or administration that remove him from empirical research, his financial prospect for the next twenty or thirty years is fairly bleak. Account also has to be taken of the 'natural history' of the research worker's intellectual career; although there are brilliant exceptions, it is unusual for a high level of performance to be sustained over a substantial period of time — the optimum being between the ages of about twenty-five and thirty-five years.

To harness this talent to the requirements of applied research, and of applied research in government, is a problem the solution of which has not yet been satisfactorily achieved. For it is universities which probably provide the better conditions for research, given that the number of independent research institutes for the social sciences in England, by contrast with the United States of America, is so small. And intrinsic to the idea of a university is continuity of intellectual tradition, an acceptance of the value of knowledge and the need to impart it, and the stimulus that is brought about by the fertilisation of thought within an academic discipline and between disciplines. Not everyone will share this view of scholarship and scholars, least of all W B Yeats:

> Bald heads forgetful of their sins
> Old, learned, respectable bald heads
> Edit and annotate the lines
> That young men, tossing on their beds,
> Rhymed out in love's despair
> To flatter beauty's ignorant ear.
>
> All shuffle there; all cough in ink,
> All wear the carpet with their shoes;
> All think what other people think;
> All know the man their neighbour knows.
> Lord, what would they say
> Did their Catullus walk that way?

Social science faculties are, no doubt, as intellectually incestuous as any; and it will also be recalled that some of the major works of the social sciences have been produced outside the universities: for that matter, much the same goes for the achievements of applied technology both in this century and the preceding one. Nevertheless, the increasing specialisation of knowledge, the ascendancy of the universities in the development of theory, and the relative dependence of applied social science on this development, tends to confer on these institutions a special status in a society where high value is rightly put on intellectual freedom, a freedom which includes the freedom to publish the results of research.

The commitment of the university to the pursuit of knowledge — a view necessarily simplified for the purpose of a short essay but not, it is hoped, simplistic, since it is too serious a matter in which much, potentially, is at stake — must now be contrasted with the commitment of government and its requirements for research. The most recent statement[12] on the subject sets out the general basis of government financed research and development (R. and D.) as follows:

a. Research which is not undertaken with direct application in mind but rather for the purpose of advancing knowledge is the responsibility of the scientific community. That community itself decides how the available funds should be spent in the light of its best judgement of what research is most likely to lead to fruitful discoveries, having regard to existing knowledge and scientific capability;

b. Other R. and D. is promoted by each Government Department in its area on the scale and pattern which it judges to be most appropriate to the formulation and pursuit of its policies.

The White Paper then goes on to discuss the financial arrangements whereby the Department of Education and Science channels funds to the universities on the one hand through the University Grants Committee and on the other hand through the research councils. The document also contains some account of the arrangements for R. and D. in each government department.[13]

It will be noted that the onus for the advancement of knowledge is laid on the scientific community and that, by implication, government divests itself of direct moral and practical responsibility for maintaining any particular subject or discipline except in so far as this responsibility is discharged indirectly through what is known as the 'dual support' system of University Grants Committee and research councils. It is left to individual departments to buy what they want in aid of their own policies in the open market.

What is it that departments want? At the outset — and here only the Home Office and its requirement for criminological research is under consideration — there is a distinction to be made between the expressed need of a department and the latent need; to put it crudely between what a department says it wants and what it ought to have. Demands for research may be pitched too low or too high: who is to decide what is good for a department or, to change the metaphor, the correct dosage? The answer to this is that, in a democracy, it is clearly for Ministers to lay down guidelines. These guidelines are in turn determined to a degree by financial and political constraints, and the accountability of Ministers to Parliament. In practice, the formulation of programmes of research is left to the professional and administrative advisers whose ultimate business, as civil servants, it is to execute the work. But before discussing the determination of the programme, and the nature of the investment in it — all of which constitutes the nub of technological management — further consideration should be given to the use government can put research to, and whether this use is capable of classification.

Decisions in government are normally taken within a timescale which is short. Action has to be completed today, tomorrow or by the end of the week. Government reacts to events. If the information required for any particular decision is not already available, then it has to be sought in a matter of days; at best weeks; and at worst months. The determination of certain policies may indeed take place over a longer time scale but the realities of the political cycle, and of fiscal commitment, usually mean that the absolute maximum period is three years and the realistic span little more than twelve or eighteen months. Time scales of this order do not mesh with the timing of most projects in criminological research. The mounting of a rapid survey will satisfy only a few demands: it is usually necessary to observe the effect of particular measures in which the minimum requirement may be to follow a sample of cases through the criminal process (allowing for appeals, this may exceed a year) or to collect data on the reconviction of a sample of offenders (for which a period of at least twelve months is desirable to monitor events satisfactorily). Given that few projects are completed in less than two years, the problems of co-ordinating research and decisions are therefore consider-

7

able, and it is not surprising that the tolerance of and demand for empirical research by policy makers is respectively strained and restricted. In addition, it must be emphasised that it is rare for one project to lead to or be identified positively with one policy decision; for the most part, the effect of research is cumulative and as much negative — the destruction of myths — as positive in its contribution to policy.

This presents a considerable problem to management. Few have succeeded in harnessing research to policy because what is needed is a kind of conveyor belt of continuous research from which the administrator plucks what seems relevant to the problem in hand. In these circumstances, research is certainly not likely to solve any given problem because it is neither tailored nor timed to it.[14] Furthermore, there is the likelihood that a continuous flow of research, however prestigious, will not be economical because so much of the output will have to be discarded in the sense of not being put to practical use. The benefit, in relation to cost, of such research must be low yet, in recent years, policy makers have too often had to be content to live with a situation which brings frustration to research workers who are concerned that their findings are not applied, and despair to administrators who do not get the results of research that they claim to need by a date when they can make use of them. This is not sound management practice. It was to overcome these difficulties that the principle of the policy maker as 'customer' and the social scientist as 'contractor' was introduced some years ago.[15] The customer states his requirements and the contractor carries them out. As far as criminological research in the Home Office is concerned — where the Research Unit is one of several contractors — this principle has been applied with varying degrees of success. The reasons for this are attributable partly to the intrinsic nature of the research and partly to the structural relationship of the contractor to the customer.

However research is classified — applied or pure, short-term or long-term, reactive or innovative — it is important that the contractor should be close to the customer so that fruitful co-operation may be maintained. Similar considerations apply to the formulation of programmes — as the White Paper of 1979 puts it: "One principle is common to all Home Office R. and D: the machinery for agreeing programmes of work is decentralised to the greatest possible extent."[16] All of this puts something of a burden on research workers: they are not entirely free to occupy the ivory tower of pure contemplation unsullied by the daily experience of administrative practice; they need to seek out their administrative colleagues and work alongside them in the fields without the battlements.[17] Not that many research workers lack frequent contact with, or close knowledge of, the criminal justice agencies and their clients — whether it be the police, courts, prisons and their denizens; but this is not exactly the same pasture as is tilled by administrators, and there is a danger that, in the eagerness to be helpful, social scientists neglect the policy making customer in favour of the practitioner or 'proxy customers', as these criminal justice services are sometimes described in management parlance.

8

Before pursuing the problem of structure further, it is expedient to identify the range of research that is of service to policy makers. It includes:

i. applied research that in purpose is essentially operational, as an aid to management; and is capable of being completed in six months or less;

ii. descriptive research that monitors the effect of legislation or other measures;

iii. experimental research, sometimes known as 'action research', that evaluates policy options; and

iv. fundamental research, including cohort and historical studies and other work that is likely to make a substantial contribution to theory, but which is basically long term.

Some of these categories, which are somewhat arbitrary, will overlap. The second and third categories, in particular, could be classified as having a time span that is more mid than long-term. It is to be emphasised that, whether or not any of this research helps to reduce crime, such studies can all contribute, however, to the central question which preoccupies those ultimately responsible for the criminal justice system and the services that subtend it, namely whether the distribution of resources within and between the various constituent parts is both adequate for the task and correctly balanced between competing demands.

Returning to the matter of structure, there are several points that can be made about a research capability:

i. There is no one model of capability that will suit every situation. Different countries will, indeed do, organise the management of research according to national needs and there will be, and are, variants within countries, given the differing requirements of federal and regional constitutions.

ii. Research is not an activity that can be planned by committees. It is dependent upon individual initiative and mutual trust between the sponsor and research workers, between the customer and the contractor. Committees can fix levels of investment, order priorities and help disseminate the results of research. Whether or not they include experts from outside government is a matter of choice. The alternative is to appoint independent consultants to advise the department directly.

iii. The activity should be decentralised as far as practicable and consistent with professional standards. The programme should be determined locally, subject to central review.

iv. Some central resource is needed, not only to review the programme as a whole, but to co-ordinate requirements for research, and the demands of technological management, with activities which are often the concern of separate capabilities — namely, financial and resource planning, policy analysis, and statistical and other technical services.

9

v. The capability will act as a mediator between policy makers and the scientific community. It should be in a position to sub-contract work to agencies — such as universities and polytechnics, independent institutes and commercial organisations — outside government. For this purpose it is preferable for the capability to be able to control its own budget.

vi. Consequently, and taking account of its own intramural activity, the capability should be a prime source of intelligence and information about criminological research, both at home and abroad, and any other research which has a bearing on the system of criminal justice.

vii. The capability needs the means to disseminate the results of research. This will maintain its credibility and, as crucially, the credibility of the research itself as well as the analyses of policy to which that research contributes.

The justification for a government capability of any substance is the service it provides policy makers on these counts and the extent to which it is seen as a professional resource without which the day-to-day conduct of the department would be poorer. It is the task of technological management to integrate the four categories of research listed above with the seven structural features just outlined. This is no easy task. Virtue may be rewarded but a large dowry is not the key, even if there is a minimum income on which the couple can subsist. In the past the unions so effected have run the whole gamut of marital relations and have fostered offspring legitimate and illegitimate. Time and circumstances change needs and objectives: the hallmark of any capability that expects to celebrate successive anniversaries should be flexibility.

Conclusion
This essay has considered some of the problems of harnessing knowledge about crime and criminals to policy making. It has reviewed certain principles that ought to inform the management of a government capability engaged in research for policy formation in the context of the aims implicit in a rational approach to contemporary issues in criminal justice and law enforcement. It has not attempted to evaluate the contribution that criminological research has made to the development of Home Office penal policy over the last quarter of a century — this is properly the task of an independent assessor. The impression remains, however, that the cumulative effect of what could be described as the more innovative research, backed up by substantial surveys of broad areas of study, has been instrumental in changing the attitudes and understanding of policy makers with a consequent impact on the disposal of resources.

The marriage of research and policy is indeed difficult to consummate. Whereas it is frequently assumed that both partners are in a virginal state, in practice both have been sullied by a variety of experiences. Policy making is not necessarily a rational process and research often runs ahead of issues. Social research is concerned with the identification of problems and their solutions. This essay has been at pains to point out the difficulties implicit in problem-solving in studying crime. Put another way, social research may be involved in the political assessment of the need for a policy, and is involved in the effects of a policy. This can be contentious. The product of the union between research and policy can rarely be delivered without the aid of several midwives, including public opinion.

In the immediate future, resources are unlikely to be less constrained and the problems intrinsic to, and impinging on, the criminal justice system are unlikely to diminish and become less importunate. Doubt about the human predicament but belief in an ultimately rational world should reinforce support for scientific research. So no apology is made for letting Alexander Pope have the last word:

> A little learning is a dang'rous thing;
> Drink deep, or taste not the Pierian spring:
> There shallow draughts intoxicate the brain,
> And drinking largely sobers us again.

Notes

1. The quotations are drawn, respectively, from: I. Berlin: *Four Essays on Liberty* Oxford, 1969; and *Russian Thinkers*. Penguin Books, Harmondsworth, 1979. In Turgenev's novel, Bazarov, a radical, is contrasted with the Kirsanov family, the equivalent of conservative, landed gentry but not without liberal tendencies.

2. John Croft: *Research in Criminal Justice*. Home Office Research Study No. 44. Her Majesty's Stationery Office, London, 1978.

3. John Croft: *Research and Criminal Policy*. Home Office Research Study No. 59. Her Majesty's Stationery Office, London, 1980.

4. The reader is referred to recent works, mainly by social historians: for example, the volume edited by V. A. C. Gatrell, Bruce Lenman and Geoffrey Parker, *Crime and the Law. The Social History of Crime in Western Europe since 1500*. Europa publications, London, 1980. The bibliographical essay by Victor Bailey on *Crime, Criminal Justice and Authority in England* in *Society for the Study of Labour History* (Bulletin No. 40, Spring, 1980) gives a useful summary of reference.

5. In the present decade of the twentieth century, the only industrialised countries of the western world to have avoided the consequence of an increasing crime rate and industrial development are apparently Japan and Switzerland. Some evidence is accumulating, however, that crime rates may be waxing even in Japan.

6. Further historical and empirical research is needed. As to the former, no doubt the completion of three projects — all funded by the Home Office — namely a fifth volume of Sir Leon Radzinowicz's *A History of English Criminal Law and its Administration from 1750* (in which, in collaboration with Dr. Roger Hood, the narrative will be continued to 1914), a study, by Dr. Victor Bailey, of English criminal policy between the wars, and Dr. Sean McConville's research into penal ideas and prison management in the later part of the nineteenth century and the first half of the twentieth century will contribute to understanding of the principal weapons in the armour of law enforcement and control.

It would be useful to know more about the relationship between the official rate of crime — as recorded by the police, the courts and other agencies — and the 'real' rate of crime (the so-called 'dark figure') — as recorded by victims and offenders themselves; and furthermore how this changes over time and what cultural or other patterns it reflects. The Home Office is considering the practicality of research in this area.

7. This essay does not cover considerable advances made in physical prevention and forensic detection of crime; of themselves, however, these are insufficient to do more perhaps, than contain crime. For another aspect of technical management, see the critique of computerised aids to law enforcement by Mike Hough in *Home Office Research Bulletin No. 10* (1980) — 'Information technology and police management'.

8. But see volume one of *Comparative Criminology* by Hermann Mannheim published by Routledge and Kegan Paul, London, 1965 (Chapter 3, p.79 *et seq.* in particular).

9. There is some discussion of this topic, in terms of conflict and consensus theory, by Lynn McDonald in *The Sociology of Law and Order*, Faber and Faber, London, 1976.

10. Manipulation of the criminal code and penal practice by the corporate state is the bane of this century. Indeed it is a temptation for any absolute power, however manifested; the constitution of the United States of America is specifically designed to prevent such usurpation.

Some aspects of the Nazi attitude are discussed in Hermann Mannheim's *Group Problems in Crime and Punishment*, Routledge and Kegan Paul, London, 1955 (p.50 *et seq.*).

11. The report by the US National Academy of Sciences — *Understanding Crime: an evaluation of the National Institute of Law Enforcement and Justice*, Washington DC, 1977 — is an important document. A report for the Council of Europe by Dr Franco Ferracuti, *The Co-ordination of Research and the Application of its Findings in the Field of Criminal Policy*, was published (mimeograph) by the European Committee on Crime Problems at Strasbourg in 1979; it contains a bibliography. To those references which are to be found on page 10 of Home Office Research Study No.44 should be added Home Office Research Unit Bulletin No.6, 1978 and an article by R. M. Morris, head of the Home Office Crime Policy Planning Unit, entitled 'Home Office crime policy planning: six years on' and published in the *Howard Journal*, Vol XIX, No.3, 1980.

12. Lord Privy Seal: *Review of the Framework for Government Research and Development (Cmnd.5046)*. Cmnd 7499. Her Majesty's Stationery Office, London (March) 1979.

13. The arrangements for the Home Office are described on pages 41 and 42 *op.cit.*

14. Nevertheless *The Royal Commission on Criminal Procedure*, which was appointed in February 1978 and reported (Cmnd. 8092: Her Majesty's Stationery Office, London) in January 1981, succeeded in processing research (the results of which were published in nine volumes in advance of the main report) that could be incorporated in the argument that supported the Commission's findings.

15. *Framework for Government Research and Development*. Cmnd.5046. Her Majesty's Stationery Office, London, 1972. See also the discussion on pages 8 and 9 of Home Office Research Study No.44 *op.cit.*

16. Page 41 *op.cit.*

17. It is curious how agricultural metaphors still pervade the language. A project that 'covers the ground' is carried out 'in the field', a 'rich harvest' of results may be obtained although there are many 'furrows to be ploughed', and so forth.

Publications

Titles already published for the Home Office

Postage extra

Studies in the Causes of Delinquency and the Treatment of Offenders

1. Prediction methods in relation to borstal training. Hermann Mannheim and Leslie T. Wilkins. 1955. vi+276pp. (11 340051 9) £3.
2. †Time spent awaiting trial. Evelyn Gibson. 1960. 46pp. (34-368-2) 27p.
3. †Delinquent generations. Leslie T. Wilkins. 1960. 20pp. (11 340053 5) 16p.
4. Murder. Evelyn Gibson and S. Klein. 1961. 44pp. (11 340054 3) 30p.
5. Persistent criminals. A study of all offenders liable to preventive detention in 1956. W. H. Hammond and Edna Chayen. 1963.x+238pp. (34-368-5) £1.25.
6. Some statistical and other numerical techniques for classifying individuals. P. McNaughton-Smith. 1965.34pp. (34-368-6) 17½p.
7. Probation research: a preliminary report. Part I. General outline of research. Part II. Study of Middlesex probation area (SOMPA). Steven Folkard, Kate Lyon, Margaret M. Carver and Erica O'Leary. 1966. vi+58pp. (11 340374 7) 42p.
8. †Probation research: national study of probation. Trends and regional comparisons in probation (England and Wales). Hugh Barr and Erica O'Leary. 1966. viii+52pp. (34-368-8) 25p.
9. †Probation research. A survey of group work in the probation service. Hugh Barr. 1966. viii+96pp. (34-368-9) 40p.
10. †Types of delinquency and home background. A validation study of Hewitt and Jenkins' hypothesis. Elizabeth Field. 1967. vi+22pp. (34-368-10) 14p.
11. †Studies of female offenders. No. 1 — Girls of 16-20 years sentenced to borstal or detention centre training in 1963. No 2. — Women offenders in the Metropolitan Police District in March and April 1957. No 3. — A description of women in prison on January 1, 1965. Nancy Goodman and Jean Price. 1967. vi+78pp. (34-368-11) 30p.
12. †The use of the Jesness Inventory on a sample of British probationers. Martin Davies. 1967. iv+20pp. (34-368-12) 11p.
13. The Jesness Inventory: application to approved school boys. Joy Mott. 1969. iv+28pp. (11 340063 2) 17½p.

Home Office Research Studies

1. Workloads in children's departments. Eleanor Grey. 1969. vi+75pp. (11 340101 9) 37½p.
2. †Probationers in their social environment. A study of male probationers aged 17-20, together with an analysis of those reconvicted within twelve months. Martin Davies. 1969. vii+204pp. (11 340102 7) 87½p.
3. Murder 1957 to 1968. A Home Office Statistical Division report on murder in England and Wales. Evelyn Gibson and S. Klein (with annex by the Scottish Home and Health Department on murder in Scotland). 1969. vi+94pp. (11 340103 5) 60p.

---

†Out of print. Photostat copies can be purchased from Her Majesty's Stationery Office upon request.

4. Firearms in crime. A Home Office Statistical Division report on indictable offences involving firearms in England and Wales. A. D. Weatherhead and B. M. Robinson. 1970. viii+37pp. (11 340104 3) 30p.

5. †Financial penalties and probation. Martin Davies. 1970. vii+38pp. (11 340105 1) 30p.

6. Hostels for probationers. Study of the aims, working and variations in the effectiveness of male probation hostels with special reference to the influence of the environment on delinquency. Ian Sinclair. 1971. iv+199pp. (11 340106 X) £1.15.

7. Prediction methods in criminology including a prediction study of young men on probation. Frances H. Simon. 1971. xi+233pp. (11 340107 8) £1.25.

8. †Study of the juvenile liaison scheme in West Ham 1961-1965. Marilyn Taylor. 1971. vi+45pp. (11 340108 6) 35p.

9. Explorations in after-care. I—After-care units in London, Liverpool and Manchester. Martin Silberman (Royal London Prisoners' Aid Society), Brenda Chapman. II—After-care hostels receiving a Home Office grant. Ian Sinclair and David Snow (HORU). III—St Martin of Tours House, Aryeh Leissner (National Burea for Co-operation in Child Care). 1971. xi+168pp. (11 340109 4) 85p.

10. A survey of adoption in Great Britain. Eleanor Grey in collaboration with R. M. Blunden. 1971. ix+168pp. (11 340110 8) 95p.

11. †Thirteen-year-old approved school boys in 1962. Elizabeth Field, W. H. Hammond and J. Tizard. 1971. ix+45pp. (11 340111 6) 35p.

12. Absconding from approved schools. R. V. G. Clarke and D. N. Martin. 1971. vi+145pp. (11 340112 4) 85p.

13. An experiment in personality assessment of young men remanded in custody. H. Sylvia Anthony. 1972. viii+79pp. (11 340113 2) 52½p.

14. Girl offenders aged 17-20 years. I—Statistics relating to girl offenders aged 17-20 years from 1960 to 1970. II—Re-offending by girls released from borstal or detention centre training. III—The problems of girls released from borstal training during their period on after-care. Jean Davies and Nancy Goodman. 1972. v+77pp. (11 340114 0) 52½p.

15. †The controlled trial in institutional research — paradigm or pitfall for penal evaluators? R.V.G. Clarke and D. B. Cornish. 1972. v+33pp. (11 340115 9) 29p.

16. A survey of fine enforcement. Paul Softley. 1973. v+65pp. (11 340116 7) 47p.

17. †An index of social environment designed for use in social work research. Martin Davies. 1973. v+61pp. (11 340117 5) 47p.

18. †Social enquiry reports and the probation service. Martin Davies and Andrea Knopf. 1973. v+47pp. (11 340118 3) 50p.

19. †Depression, psychopathic personality and attempted suicide in a borstal sample. H. Sylvia Anthony. 1973. viii+44pp. (0 11 340119 1) 36½p.

20. The use of bail and custody by London magistrates' courts before and after the Criminal Justice Act 1967. Frances Simon and Mollie Weatheritt. 1974. vi+78pp. (0 11 340120 5) 57p.

21. Social work in the environment. A study of one aspect of probation practice. Martin Davies, with Margaret Rayfield, Alaster Calder and Tony Fowles. 1974. x+164pp. (0 11 340121 3) £1.10.

22. Social work in prisons. An experiment in the use of extended contact with offenders. Margaret Shaw. 1974. viii+156pp. (0 11 340122 1) £1.45.

23. Delinquency amongst opiate users. Joy Mott and Marilyn Taylor. 1974. vi+54pp. (0 11 340663 0) 41p.

24. IMPACT. Intensive matched probation and after-care treatment. Vol.1. The design of the probation experiment and an interim evaluation. M. S. Folkard, A. J. Fowles, B. C. McWilliams, W. McWilliams, D. D. Smith, D. E. Smith and G. R. Walmsley. 1974. vi+54pp. (0 11 340664 9) £1.25.

---

†Out of print. Photostat copies can be purchased from Her Majesty's Stationery Office upon request.

25. The approved school experience. An account of boys' experience of training under differing regimes of approved schools, with an attempt to evaluate the effectiveness of that training. Anne B. Dunlop. 1974. viii+124pp. (0 11 340665 7) £1.22.

26. Absconding from open prisons. Charlotte Banks, Patricia Mayhew and R. J. Sapsford. 1975. viii+92pp. (0 11 340666 5) 95p.

27. Driving while disqualified. Sue Kriefman. 1975. vi+138pp. (0 11 340667 3) £1.22.

28. Some male offenders' problems. I—Homeless offenders in Liverpool. W. McWilliams. II—Casework with short-term prisoners. Julie Holborn. 1975. x+150pp. (0 11 340668 1) £2.50.

29. Community service orders. K. Pease, P. Durkin, I. Earnshaw, D. Payne and J. Thorpe. 1975. viii+80pp. (0 11 340669 X) 75p.

30. Field Wing Bail Hostel: the first nine months. Frances Simon and Sheena Wilson. 1975. viii+56pp. (0 11 340670 3) 85p.

31. Homicide in England and Wales 1967-1971. Evelyn Gibson. 1975. iv+60pp. (0 11 340753 X) 90p.

32. Residential treatment and its effects on delinquency. D. B. Cornish and R. V. G. Clarke. 1975. vi+74pp. (0 11 340672 X) £1.00.

33. Further studies of female offenders. Part A: Borstal girls eight years after release. Nancy Goodman, Elizabeth Maloney and Jean Davies. Part B: The sentencing of women at the London Higher Courts. Nancy Goodman, Paul Durkin and Janet Halton. Part C: Girls appearing before a juvenile court. Jean Davies. 1976. vi+114pp. (0 11 340673 8) £1.55.

34. Crime as opportunity. P. Mayhew, R. V. G. Clarke, A. Sturman and J. M. Hough. 1976. vii+36pp. (0 11 340674 6) 70p.

35. The effectiveness of sentencing: a review of the literature. S. R. Brody. 1976. v+89pp. (0 11 340675 4) £1.15.

36. IMPACT. Intensive matched probation and after-care treatment. Vol. II—The results of the experiment. M. S. Folkard, D. E. Smith and D. D. Smith. 1976. xi+40pp. (0 11 340676 2) 80p.

37. Police cautioning in England and Wales. J. A. Ditchfield. 1976. iv+31pp. (0 11 340677 0) 65p.

38. Parole in England and Wales. C. P. Nuttall, with E. E. Barnard, A. J. Fowles, A. Frost, W. H. Hammond, P. Mayhew, K. Pease, R. Tarling and M. J. Weatheritt. 1977. vi+90pp. (0 11 340678 9) £1.75.

39. Community service assessed in 1976. K. Pease, S. Billingham and I. Earnshaw. 1977. vi+29pp. (0 11 340679 7) 75p.

40. Screen violence and film censorship. Stephen Brody. 1977. vi+179pp. (0 11 340680 0) £2.75.

41. Absconding from borstals. Gloria K. Laycock. 1977. v+82pp. (0 11 340681 9) £1.50.

42. Gambling—a review of the literature and its implications for policy and research. D. B. Cornish. 1978. xii+284pp. (0 11 340682 7) £4.25.

43. Compensation orders in magistrates' courts. Paul Softley. 1978. vi+41pp. (0 11 340683 5) 90p.

44. Research in criminal justice. John Croft. 1978. vi+16pp. (0 11 340684 3) 50p.

45. Prison welfare: an account of an experiment at Liverpool. A. J. Fowles. 1978. v+34pp. (0 11 340685 1) 75p.

46. Fines in magistrates' courts. Paul Softley. 1978. v+42pp. (0 11 340686 X) £1.00.

47. Tackling vandalism. R. V. G. Clarke (editor), F. J. Gladstone, A. Sturman and Sheena Wilson (contributors). 1978. vi+91pp. (0 11 340687 8) £2.00.

48. Social inquiry reports: a survey. Jennifer Thorpe. 1979. vi+55pp. (0 11 340688 6) £1.50.

49. Crime in public view. P. Mayhew, R. V. G. Clarke, J. N. Burrows, J. M. Hough and S. W. C. Winchester. 1979. v+36pp. (0 11 340689 4) £1.00.

50. Crime and the community. John Croft. 1979. v+16pp. (0 11 340690 8) 65p.

51. Life-sentence prisoners. David Smith (editor), Christopher Brown, Joan Worth, Roger Sapsford and Charlotte Banks (contributors). 1979. v+52pp. (0 11 340691 6) £1.25.

52. Hostels for offenders. Jane E. Andrews with an appendix by Bill Sheppard. 1979. v+30pp. (0 11 240692 4) £1.50.

16

53. Previous convictions, sentence and reconviction: a statistical study of a sample of 5,000 offenders convicted in January 1971. G. J. O. Phillpotts and L. B. Lancucki. 1979. v+55pp. (0 11 340693 2) £2.25.

54. Sexual offences, consent and sentencing. Roy Walmsley and Karen White. 1979. vi+77pp. (0 11 340649 0) £2.75.

55. Crime prevention and the police. John Burrows, Paul Ekblom and Kevin Heal. 1979. v+37pp. (0 11 340695 9) £1.75.

56. Sentencing practice in magistrates' courts. Roger Tarling with the assistance of Mollie Weatheritt. 1979. vii+54pp. (0 11 340696 7) £2.25.

57. Crime and comparative research. John Croft. 1979. vi+16pp. (0 11 340697 5) £1.00.

58. Race, crime and arrests. Philip Stevens and Carole F. Wills. 1979. v+69pp. (0 11 340698 3) £2.75.

59. Research and criminal policy. John Croft. 1980. iv+14pp. (0 11 340699 1) £1.75.

60. Junior attendance centres. Anne B. Dunlop. 1980. v+47pp. (0 11 340700 9) £2.75.

61. Police interrogation: an observational study in four police stations. Paul Sotfley with the assistance of David Brown, Bob Forde, George Mair and David Moxon. 1980. vii+67pp. (0 11 340701 7) £3.90.

62. Co-ordinating crime prevention efforts. F. J. Gladstone. 1980. v+74pp. (0 11 340702 5) £3.90.

63. Crime prevention publicity: an assessment. D. Riley and P. Mayhew. 1980. v+47pp. (0 11 340703 3) £3.30.

64. Taking offenders out of circulation. Stephen Brody and Roger Tarling. 1980. v+46pp. (0 11 340704 1) £3.00.

65. Alcoholism and social policy: are we on the right lines? Mary Tuck. 1980. v+30pp. (0 11 340705 X) £2.70.

66. Persistent petty offenders. Suzan Fairhead. 1981. vi+78pp. (0 11 340706 8) £3.90.

67. Crime control and the police. Kevin Heal and Pauline Morris. 1981. iv+66pp. (0 11 340707 6) £3.60.

68. Ethnic minorities in Britain: a study of trends in their position since 1961. Simon Field, George Mair, Tom Rees and Philip Stevens. 1981. iv+48pp. (0 11 340208 4) £3.60.

HMSO

The above publications can be purchased from the Government Bookshops at the addresses listed on cover page iv (post orders to PO Box 569, London SE1 9NH) or through booksellers.

The following Home Office research publications are available on request from the Home Office Research Unit, Information Section, 50 Queen Anne's Gate, London, SW1H 9AT.

Research Unit Papers

1. Uniformed police work and management technology. J. M. Hough. 1980.

2. Supplementary information on sexual offences and sentencing. Roy Walmsley and Karen White. 1980.

Research Bulletin

The Research Bulletin is published twice a year and consists mainly of short articles relating to projects which are part of the Home Office Research Unit's research programme.

Printed in England for Her Majesty's Stationery Office by Linneys of Mansfield
Dd 716594 C17 5/81